Katharine HEPBURN

Jessica Hodge

MAGNA BOOKS

Published by Magna Books
Magna Road
Wigston
Leicester LE8 2ZH

Produced by Bison Books Ltd
Kimbolton House
117A Fulham Road
London SW3 6RL

ISBN 1-85422-298-8

Printed in Hong Kong

Page 1: A studio shot of Hepburn in 1944, the year she
made *Dragon Seed*, based on Pearl S Buck's best-selling
novel, in which she plays a Chinese peasant girl. It is
one of her less convincing roles, though immensely
popular with wartime audiences.

Page 2: Kate still glamorous in the 1960s.

Right: Kate arrives back in Hollywood in November
1932. When her first film role in *A Bill of Divorcement*
was acclaimed by the critics, she was summoned back
from Europe, where she and husband Ludlow Ogden
Smith had gone in the hope of rescuing their failing
marriage.

Far right: Kate in the stage production of *The Warrior's
Husband* in 1930.

Contents

Right: Another early publicity shot taken on Kate's first arrival in Hollywood in 1932, this time looking vampish with that regular Hollywood prop, the cigarette. She was intensely impatient of Hollywood habits and the need to play at being a star. In her first confrontation with RKO's press department, she told them that her private life was her own and she did not believe in publicity. The studio did not for many months learn that she was married, and instead wild rumors abounded of a lesbian relationship with Laura Harding. The press soon scented the fact that a new star was rising on the set of RKO's latest picture, *A Bill of Divorcement*, however, and visiting reporters were delighted by Kate's appearance between takes in her ancient dungarees. RKO were much more disapproving and the offending garment was removed from her dressing room. Kate threatened to walk through the lot naked to retrieve them and when her bluff was called did indeed, as she later recalled, 'walk through the lot in my underpants.' The dungarees were returned but all pictures of the exploit were confiscated.

an actress. It was not until *The African Queen* in 1951 that she found a solo role worthy of her talents and embarked on a new phase both on screen and stage. The year 1952 found her on stage in London performing in George Bernard Shaw, 1955 saw her touring Australia in Shakespeare. Her swansong with Tracy was *Guess Who's Coming to Dinner*, which won her a second Oscar 34 years after the first, and after his death in 1967 she went on to star in two more Oscar-winning film roles and a musical, *Coco*. She finally emerged from her cocoon of privacy in the 1980s to write both about her relationship with Tracy and the making of *The African Queen*, which she regarded as a pivotal role, while in 1991 she reviewed her life in characteristically energetic and breathless style in her autobiography, *Me, Stories of My Life*, which ends with the two words 'Yes, lucky.'

The family into which Katharine Houghton Hepburn was born on November 8th, 1907 (not 1909 as some chroniclers have it), was no ordinary one. Both her parents were formidable, committed, independent-minded individuals. Dr Thomas Norval Hepburn, son of an Episcopalian minister, was a medical student when he first met Kit Houghton. Originally from Scotland, the Hepburns could trace their ancestry back to James Hepburn, Earl of Bothwell, third husband of Mary Queen of Scots. Tom Hepburn was a natural athlete, and physical fitness was a lifelong obsession which he passed on to his oldest daughter; he believed that a lazy body produced a lazy mind. A well-built, red-headed man with a booming Virginian voice, he was enough of an original that the strong-minded Kit Houghton said as soon as she met him: 'That's the one.'

Katharine Martha Houghton was a member of the rich and socially prominent Bostonian Houghton family. In 1892, when she was 13, her father committed suicide and her mother died soon after of cancer; the three Houghton sisters were subsequently supported by their maternal uncle. All three upstanding young women, they insisted, much to their uncle's shock, on attending Bryn Mawr, then regarded as the most academic of the women's colleges, and getting an education – Kit, as she was invariably known, with the stated intention of 'raising hell with established customs.' By the time she met Tom Hepburn she had already been to France with a girlfriend, sailing with a mere ten dollars in her pocket because her uncle disapproved and withheld her allowance.

Married in 1904, the Hepburns remained a devoted couple for nearly 50 years, until Kit's death in 1951. Their daughter has on many occasions been quoted as saying 'I don't believe in marriage . . . possibly the only happy marriage I've known was my parents'. They never argued about things . . . they only argued about ideas.' The Hepburns began their married life in Hartford, Connecticut, where Tom moved from an internship at the Hartford Hospital to a general surgical practice specializing in urology, then a very young science. As he prospered in his profession, Dr Hepburn was able to move his young family to more spacious and elegant accommodation, and Katharine – Kathy at first to her family, Red-

Left: Katharine Martha Hepburn, Kate's mother, with her two younger daughters Marion (center) and Margaret, arriving in London in 1935. Kate has written in her autobiography that from her mother she learnt: 'Don't give in. Fight for your future. *Independence* is the only solution. Women are as good as men. Onward!'

top to her father alone, who was delighted with his red-headed daughter – was born in a comfortable house on Hawthorne Street. Soon after her birth, Kit Hepburn, at the urging of her husband who felt that she needed more stimulation, attended a lecture by Emmeline Pankhurst, the British suffragette.

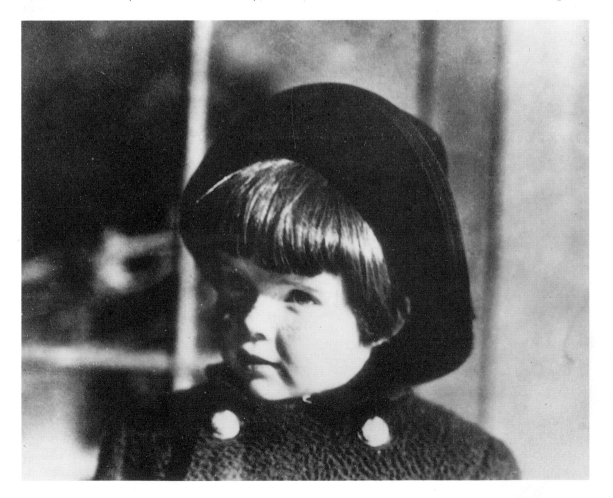

Left: Kate aged four. From her earliest years her father encouraged her to be a gymnast. She could stand and walk on her hands, turn handsprings and take a flying somersault off her father's shoulders. She writes 'I was standing on my head the other day and I got to thinking how probably unusual it is for someone of my age to do this.'

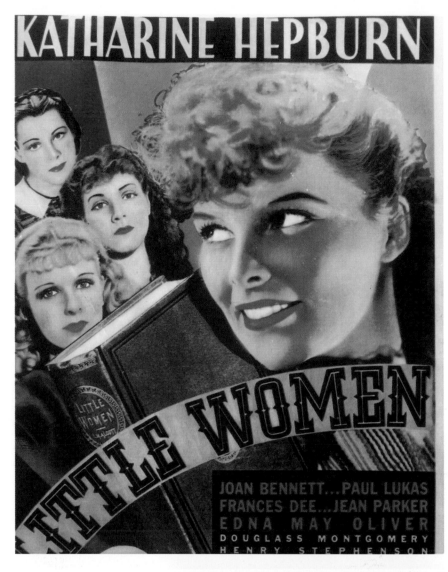

KATHARINE HEPBURN

LITTLE WOMEN

JOAN BENNETT...PAUL LUKAS
FRANCES DEE...JEAN PARKER
EDNA MAY OLIVER
DOUGLASS MONTGOMERY
HENRY STEPHENSON

Above: Publicity poster for *Little Women* (1933), one of Hepburn's own favorite movies.

establishing from the very beginning of her initially tempestuous relationship with Hollywood her determination that she should call the shots. She chose a scene from *Holiday*, already her favorite play, ensuring that she was at ease with her material, unlike most screen tests.

RKO at the time were casting *A Bill of Divorcement*, a Clemence Dane play about the daughter who abandons her own happiness in order to care for her once-great but now unbalanced composer father. John Barrymore had already been cast as the father and the young and promising George Cukor hired to direct, but David O Selznick at RKO was not convinced by any of the frontrunners for the role of Sydney Fairfield, who included Norma Shearer, Irene Dunne and Anita Louise. Hepburn's screen test decided him; as Cukor recalled, it was 'quite unlike any test I had ever seen before. Though she'd never made a movie, she seemed to have this very definite knowledge and feeling right from the start.' Still unsure about Hollywood, Kate made Hayward demand $1500 a week, an amazing sum for a newcomer and, even more amazingly, RKO agreed.

When Kate arrived in Los Angeles on July 1st, 1932, with Laura Harding for moral support, Cukor and Selznick were initially appalled at their rashness. As usual she was recklessly dressed, brusque and apparently self-confident in manner, although undeniably distinctive. She behaved like a star before she be-

Right: Kate with David Manners as the fiancé she sends away in order to care for her mentally tortured father, in her first film, *A Bill of Divorcement* (1932). According to *The New York Herald Tribune*, she 'is both beautiful and distinguished as the daughter, and seems definitely established for an important cinema career.'

Left: Publicity poster for *Break of Hearts* (1935). Kate and Charles Boyer were both praised for their respective roles as aspiring but unknown composer and eminent conductor but the film was not a success. They fall in love and marry; she leaves him when he deceives her with another woman, but returns with noble self-sacrifice when alcoholism threatens his career. The 'cheap emotionalism and shallow psychology' of the script was panned by the critics.

Below: Movie star Hepburn on the cover of *Screenland* magazine.

came one; on her first day she arrived for work in a huge chauffeur-driven hired car, dressed in a much-too-large sweater pinned together at the back and a pair of baggy pants. She and Cukor had an almost immediate confrontation over her wardrobe but Cukor stood firm and in the end it was Kate who backed down. She developed an intense respect for his judgment as a director and they also became close and lasting friends; Tracy rented a cottage on Cukor's estate for the duration of his liaison with Hepburn, and Hepburn and Cukor continued to work together sporadically for nearly 50 years. From the beginning she had a way with the movie camera, and Cukor knew how to use it. Her very first appearance in *A Bill of Divorcement*, a long tracking shot in which she silently descends a staircase, made it clear that Cukor was introducing a new star. And after some initial upsets with Barrymore, who made his inevitable pass and was equally inevitably rebuffed, Kate established a warm and educational relationship with her co-star, saying later that 'He taught me all that he could pour into one greenhorn in that short time.' The critics thought well both of the film and of Hepburn, and RKO heaved a corporate sigh of relief.

Kate's contract with RKO gave the company the option of keeping her, which Selznick now exercised, but it also guaranteed Kate her freedom for seven months of the year, when she inevitably gravitated eastward, back to family, friends and Fenwick. She never felt at home in Hollywood and never bought a house there. Her next film, *Christopher Strong,*

The Smart Screen Magazine

SCREENLAND

May

15c
20c in Canada

Katharine Hepburn

NEW CONTEST!
Gifts from
**MARION DAVIES,
CLARK GABLE, HELEN HAYES, MYRNA LOY,
JEAN PARKER, MADGE EVANS**—See Page 20

Above: Kate as the career-minded aviatrix who falls in love with a married man in *Christopher Strong* (1933), her second film.

was generally reckoned a bitter disappointment after the success of *A Bill of Divorcement*. It cast Kate as a flying ace who has a passionate affair with a married man, becomes pregnant by him but keeps the pregnancy a secret, and ultimately kills herself by pulling off her oxygen mask while breaking the world altitude record. Already, in her first starring role, she had established herself as the independent free-thinking woman she was to continue to

play with variations throughout her life. For modern audiences this is part of her appeal but it was an image that fitted less easily into the 1930s. *Christopher Strong* was also interesting for its pairing of feminist star with feminist director, Dorothy Arzner, but unfortunately the relationship was less than successful. Kate was not the first choice for the film and Arzner resented the change, made just as shooting was about to start. And Kate reacted badly to

Arzner's demanding and autocratic way of working.

After one hit and one flop in her first six months, Kate went on to score a resounding success with her next RKO movie, *Morning Glory*, which won her her first Oscar. A wonderfully cliché-ridden piece which hardly bears watching today, this was loosely based on the story of Tallulah Bankhead, the classic tale of the smalltown girl who walks on to the stage an unknown and comes back a star – *42nd Street* without the songs. The screenplay was generally considered artificial, and Adolphe Menjou as the producer and Douglas Fairbanks Jr as a lovelorn playwright are neither of them at their best, but there was no doubt about Kate. The London *Times* reported that 'in a depressingly second-rate story she admirably mingles intellectual austerity with physical gaucherie,' while *Time* magazine acknowledged that:

From this immemorial fairy tale the delicate, muscled face of Heroine Hepburn shines out like a face on a coin. Of the brash little provincial she makes a strangely distinguished character, a little mad from hunger and dreams, absurdly audacious and trusting. Since *Christoper Strong* she has toned down her strident voice, taken off some of her angular swank in gesture and strut, found other ways to register emotion than by dilating her nostrils.

A reception like this guaranteed an Oscar nomination and the competition was none too strong. Although *Morning Glory* earned no other awards, it did get Kate the first of her four

Oscars without too much difficulty. Ironic that this was for one of her least characteristic parts as the girl from nowhere.

Above: A boyish Hepburn in her dressing room, with hair cut short for *Christopher Strong*. Clearly she had been earmarked for 'strong drama'; although some critics praised the movie, audiences were disappointed after the more immediate appeal of *A Bill of Divorcement*.

Left: Kate in *Morning Glory* (1933) as the earnest, idealistic and determined Eva Lovelace, the New England girl who arrives in New York to conquer the stage. After anguish and disappointment, and a sensation at a Broadway party when she gets drunk on champagne and recites Hamlet's soliloquy, she makes it to the top. As did Kate: the role won her her first Oscar.

possible. She fought senselessly with practically everyone from top producers to lowest technicians. She was insulting and abusive to the press and gave out ridiculous and inane interviews in which she deliberately distorted the facts of her private life. She allowed herself to be photographed without make-up, in all her freckles, and even worse she dressed hideously in mannish garb – sloppy slacks, sweaters and men's trousers and suits. She hired a Rolls Royce to take her to the studio and she read her fan mail sitting on the curb outside the RKO lot.

None of this seems very heinous today, and much of it was Hepburn simply being herself, always an important part of her charm and success. Some of it was also due to the pressure under which films were made; most of Kate's early pictures were made in four weeks, *Morning Glory* in a staggering 18 days, which ruled out doing much other than getting up in front of the cameras and acting. Some of the legendary bad behavior was due to the terror she felt at first in going before the cameras; it was only with *Morning Glory* that she began to feel at ease with the camera and recognized how it enhanced her striking, unconventional looks. But there was also a real ambivalence in Hepburn at this stage in her career that Hollywood recognized and resented – stars were not supposed to be half-hearted in their allegiance to the system which had made them. On the one hand she demanded privacy, on the other she behaved in a way guaranteed to draw attention, with her mannish clothes and unorthodox escapades with Laura Harding. It was as if coming west was in some way equivalent to being let out of school and she was celebrating an adolescence that had been pre-empted by Tom's death. And the vaunted independence did not extend to financial matters. Soon after arriving in Hollywood, Kate confessed to her father that she had already spent her salary. Dr Hepburn was furious and insisted that she send him her checks and he would send her an adequate allowance, an arrangement that continued until his death. Her family remained intensely important and she returned east whenever she could to spend recuperative time at Fenwick. Years later she recalled her early days:

I became a star before I knew how to be a star, and then I thought, well, maybe I'd better learn how to do it. The first thing to learn is that nobody must ever know how terrified you are.

As the marriage with Luddy foundered, Kate found herself drawn into a closer relationship with her agent Leland Hayward, who was to remain the most influential man in her life, other than her father, until the advent of Spencer Tracy. Hayward was an unusually urbane and cultivated figure for Hollywood, scion of a well-established Nebraska family who had attended Princeton. He had married

Opposite: A haunted and vulnerable looking Hepburn with Doug Fairbanks Jr, her co-star in *Morning Glory.*

Left: A much retouched photo of Kate with Leland Hayward (sometimes wrongly identified as Luddy). In her autobiography, she writes: 'Life with Leland had no problems. . . There were solutions to everything. Joy was the constant mood. . . we had such fun.'

Below: In April 1934 the marriage to Luddy finally ended; in this delightfully casual shot, Kate is seen with Laura Harding visiting the ruins of Uxmal on the Yucatan peninsula, Mexico, where she obtained a divorce.

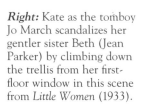

Right: Kate as the tomboy Jo March scandalizes her gentler sister Beth (Jean Parker) by climbing down the trellis from her first-floor window in this scene from *Little Women* (1933).

Below: 'As an antidote to the febrile dramas of the underworld and backstage musical spectacles, *Little Women* comes as a reminder that emotions and vitality and truth can be evoked from lavender and lace as well as from machine guns and precision dances.' – *New York Post*

Texan heiress Lola Gibbs, divorced and then remarried her before he met Kate, and included some of Hollywood's most glamorous ladies, notably Ginger Rogers, Miriam Hopkins and, later, Margaret Sullavan among his clients. He was given to strolling through the executive offices of the movie world in white flannels and yachting sneakers, and requesting, and getting, outrageous salaries for his clients. He both liked and respected strong, clever women, and it was he more than anyone who helped Kate to overcome her nervy, self-defensive reaction to Hollywood hype, and to develop her own distinctive style both on and off screen. Hayward was not the only man to yearn after Kate, however; Doug Fairbanks, Jr, with whom she starred in *Morning Glory*, spent three months trying to persuade her to have dinner with him, only to have her plead a headache halfway through.

It was Hayward who, after the success of *Morning Glory*, managed to get Kate back with two film-makers who really understood her, Selznick and Cukor. They were in the process of scripting a screen version of *Little Women*, Louisa M Alcott's classic story of four sisters growing up during the Civil War. Cukor felt that 'like Garbo and *Camille*, (Kate) was born to play Jo. She's tender and funny, fiercely loyal, and plays the fool when she feels like it. There's a purity about her. Kate and Jo are the same girl . . .' Which of course was largely true; Kate's upbringing had been filled with just the same 'admirable New England sternness', and she threw herself into filming with a fervor that

cemented her already successful partnership with Cukor. Not that they didn't row, and once he even hit her after she had ruined an essential costume by spilling icecream down it, but their mutual respect survived and was strengthened by these exchanges. For the first time, too, Kate established a good relationship with the film crew and was delighted when, after a particularly outrageous bit of overacting on her part, a large ham was solemnly lowered

from a crane and dangled before her. Cukor himself said that Kate cast 'a spell of magic, a kind of power that dominated even those scenes she's not in.' It is the first of Kate's films still to seem watchable today and her own favorite early movie, with its loose, episodic script very true to the novel, unfussy period detail and excellent playing by all concerned. According to *Time* magazine:

That *Little Women* attains so perfectly, without seeming either affected or superior, the courtesy and rueful wisdom of its original is due to expert adaptation by Sarah Y Mason and Victor Heerman [who won the film's one Oscar], to Cukor's direction and to superb acting by Katharine Hepburn.

Her next project was much less successful; she was anxious to be released by RKO so that she could take up the offer of the lead in Broadway wonder-boy Jed Harris's latest project, *The Lake,* and agreed in return to make *Spitfire* in a month for $50,000. This was a backwoods melodrama about a young tomboy faith-healer who falls in love with a dam-building engineer, feels herself deceived by him, kidnaps and cures a sick baby, but is almost lynched by her neighbors. A curious choice to follow *Little Women* and panned by the critics. *The New Yorker* said mildly that Hepburn's 'artistry does not extend to the interpretation of the primitive or the uncouth.'

Unfortunately her return to the stage was even more disastrous. It was motivated by a number of factors, not least her hurt at Leland Hayward's increasing fondness for the young Margaret Sullavan, whom he had signed six months earlier. Hepburn's relationship with Laura Harding had cooled in the course of *Little Women;* she was working too hard and well to be bothered with schoolgirl pranks and Laura returned east. Her personal life was confused and unfocused, but Luddy remained loyal and supportive. On her return to New York they moved into a large house, in which Hepburn still lives today, and she began rehearsals for *The Lake.* This was a brooding story of a passive and guilt-ridden young society woman whose husband drowns on the morning of their wedding. Noel Coward had warned Harris that the play, which had been a hit in London, would not travel well; Americans liked their heroines to be rebels not wimps, and Kate proved wholly unable to exude the necessary pathos. Harris, known as an anti-actor director, was extremely hard on her, with the result that she became confused, self-doubting and argumentative. In her autobiography, she describes the experience as 'a slow walk to the

Opposite: A relaxed and smiling Hepburn, in costume for *Alice Adams* (1935) and awaiting her cue, watches other members of the cast go through their paces with director George Stevens (in glasses).

Below: In *The Little Minister* Kate plays the glamorous Lady Babbie, who disguises herself as a gypsy and regularly visits the poor weavers in the nearby city. When the minister of the kirk falls for her, his parishioners are set to expel him – until they discover the gypsy's true identity. *The New York Times* was only moderately enthusiastic: 'Although dear Babbie's elfin whimsies are likely to cause minor teeth-gnashing among unsympathetic moderns, Miss Hepburn plays the part with likeable sprightliness and charm.'

Right: *Sylvia Scarlett* (1936) is in many ways one of the most interesting of Hepburn's early films. As the young conman to Cary Grant's stooge, she puts on a wonderful show as a starving French boy in London's Hyde Park, but draws the line at using a serving girl's affection for Grant to steal her mistress's jewels. The artist for whom she falls (Brian Aherne) is sufficiently attracted to her as a boy to invite her to sit for him, but calls her a freak of nature when he discovers her true identity. The ingenious Grant manages to engineer a happy ending for all.

gallows.' When *The Lake* opened on Broadway on the day after Christmas 1933, the only reputation that was made was that of critic Dorothy Parker, who urged her readers to go to the play to see Miss Hepburn 'run the gamut of emotion from A to B.' After 55 performances the show closed and Kate sailed on a European holiday; two months later, at the end of April 1934, she divorced Luddy.

RKO, fired by the success of *Little Women*, were anxious for Hepburn to do another costume part and offered her J M Barrie's saccharine tale *The Little Minister*, in which a Scots aristocrat disguises herself as a gypsy and falls for the local preacher. Kate was at first reluctant, until she heard that her rival Margaret Sullavan was also in the running, whereupon she went all out for the part. The indefatigable Hayward, now back on warmer terms with his unpredictable star, negotiated her a six-picture deal with RKO at $50,000 a movie, then an astronomical salary. The choice of *The Little Minister*, however, proved a real miscalculation by both Kate and RKO, who put an unprecedented $650,000 into the budget, convinced that the new puritanism of the Hays Code made schoolroom classics a safe bet. Audiences, however, much preferred the musical escapism of Astaire and Rogers to the worthy piety of a labored period romance, and the movie lost nearly $10,000.

Pandro S Berman, head of RKO production since Selznick's departure for MGM, concluded that 'Kate wasn't a movie star . . . in the

Above: Kate was just one of many actors, writers and musicians who lined up behind President Franklin D Roosevelt's New Deal. Here they meet over a fish chowder at the presidential cottage to arrange a national radio show in support of the New Deal.

Opposite: *Mary of Scotland* (1936), with Fredric March as Bothwell, was one of a series of costume melodramas which did Hepburn's career no good at all.

Left: Kate as the dreamy Alice Adams, determined to show her wealthier girl friends she can land a suitable man (Fred MacMurray). The dinner to which she invites him to meet her family is, of course, a disaster – but equally of course, all ends well. The critics acclaimed her performance as 'striking and sensitive'; 'her masterpiece to date'; and she was nominated for an Oscar.

Above: Shooting a scene from *Mary of Scotland*; director John Ford, who became a good friend, is standing left in glasses.

sense that Crawford and Shearer were actresses able to drag an audience in by their own efforts. She was a hit only in hit pictures; she couldn't save a flop. And she almost invariably chose the wrong vehicles.' A verdict that was to condition the whole of her Hollywood career. RKO's next choice was no better; costume dramas were clearly out, and instead they

cast her in a slushy and inept soap opera, *Break of Hearts*, in which a budding composer (Hepburn) abandons her promising career to save an eminent conductor (a part written for John Barrymore and finally taken by Charles Boyer) from his alcoholism.

Alice Adams, her next picture, boded little better. Based on a Booth Tarkington novel

M O PUB A37

a hit and won Kate her second Oscar nomination (the award went to Bette Davis for *Dangerous*). *Time* said grudgingly that:

Though Katharine Hepburn is possibly the least versatile of all Hollywood's leading stars, it is precisely this limitation which makes her ideal for *Alice*. The woebegone grimaces, the expressions half-childish and half-addleheaded, so startlingly misplaced in her portrayals of women of the world, are precisely those which make her portrayal of a girl she really understands her masterpiece to date.

This success guaranteed Kate freedom of choice with her next project, and she went rejoicing back to Cukor, always her favorite director. He had long wanted to film *Sylvia Scarlett*, a deliciously absurd novel by Compton Mackenzie in which the heroine disguises herself as a boy in her travels with her conman father and a cockney adventurer. Cukor believed that Kate's *garçonne* quality was perfect for the part – she later played both Shakespeare's leading cross-dressing roles in *As You Like It* and *Twelfth Night* – and Garbo had had a stunning success with *Queen Christina*, in which she also played several scenes in man's clothes, only three years before. *Sylvia Scarlett*

Below: There was much speculation about the Hepburn/Howard Hughes romance. She met him on the set of *Sylvia Scarlett* and the affair blossomed while she was on tour in *Jane Eyre*, but fizzled out after about three years. In her autobiography Hepburn writes: 'It seems to me now that we were too similar. . . We each had a wild desire to be famous. People who want to be famous are really loners.'

about a dreamy, small-town girl who pretends to be well-born and wealthy in order to catch a husband, this looked like a low-budget program-filler. Despite difficulties between director George Stevens and his wayward star, however, Kate's performance caught the pathos in this unlikely heroine and struck a nostalgic chord for her audiences. The film was

Exclusive! COMPLETE GUIDE TO ANSWERS IN $250,000 MOVIE QUIZ

ModernScreen

THE LARGEST CIRCULATION OF ANY SCREEN MAGAZINE

NOVEMBER
10 CENTS

WILL AMERICA'S HERO, HOWARD HUGHES, *Marry* KATHARINE HEPBURN?

Hedy Lamarr's LIFE STORY!

Right: *Holiday* (1938) again partnered Hepburn with Cary Grant, she trying to smooth the path for her sister and her sister's fiancé, he as the fiancé who revolts against the stuffed-shirt money-making tradition he is about to marry.

Below: Publicity still from *Holiday*. According to the *New York Daily Mirror*, 'It is a film to which Miss Hepburn is entirely suited. Surrounded by a splendid cast, placed in staggering settings and clothes, given bright dialogue which modernizes the Philip Barry play, Hepburn makes an acting carnival of *Holiday*.'

while there was a new interest in her private life in the form of reclusive millionaire Howard Hughes, whom she had first met on the set of *Sylvia Scarlett* the previous year. While *Jane Eyre* was playing in Chicago, rumors of a marriage became so strong that a large crowd waited for hours outside the County Clerk's office on January 21st, 1937, expecting Hughes to apply for a marriage license. In the end the affair fizzled out – or one version has it that Hepburn turned Hughes down – and she spent the summer at Fenwick considering her future. She was 29, had made 12 films for RKO, of which only the first four were really successful, and was now well down in the popularity stakes after four flops in a row.

In the end a reluctant return to Hollywood seemed the answer. RKO badly needed her star quality and had no other female lead of her caliber, and so offered her a generous four-film contract guaranteeing her $150,000 a film. They finally recognized that what was needed was a contemporary story, and preferably a comedy. When Kate was offered *Stage Door*, she saw at once that it was a surefire backstage drama in the same mold as the Oscar-winning *Morning Glory*. The difference was that RKO hedged their bets by adding a second leading lady, Ginger Rogers, till then known only for her partnership with Astaire, and giving Kate third billing after Rogers and Adolphe Menjou. Other members of the strong cast were Lucille Ball, Ann Miller and stage actress Constance Collier, who became a lifelong friend. The *New York Times* hailed 'the return of Miss Hepburn from farthingales and tippets.' Her director, Gregory La Cava, found her an exciting actress to work with:

To win her, to beat down that proud impervious hauteur, is a challenge only the most virile and dominant male could afford to take up. That's the sort of man who should play opposite her . . . she's never had a leading man like that. They've always let her be the master.

Prophetic words which neatly sum up Kate's predicament in Hollywood – it was to be another five years before they were fulfilled.

The re-establishment of her prestige and sense of comedy led Kate into a three-picture partnership with her old co-star Cary Grant. The first of these was Howard Hawks' classic comedy *Bringing Up Baby*, with Hepburn as a spoilt heiress with leopard in tow, who sets her heart on Cary Grant's absent-minded professor – and needless to say gets him. The earnestness she brought to the part was inspired by Hawks, who emphasized the concentrated seriousness needed to achieve true screen comedy, and it remains a distinguished and timeless delight for just that reason. But for contemporary audiences across the US it was too fast, too sophisticated, too brassy, and at the time it was a commercial failure, despite some excellent reviews.

This was bad news for RKO. Normally Hepburn's pictures could be expected to make up any American shortfall in foreign revenue because, like Dietrich, she had always been more acclaimed in Europe than at home. But with war looming things were different. This realization coincided with the publication of an Independent Theater Owners of America list of all those screen artists considered to be 'box office poison'. The list included many of the best and most famous actors of the day: Garbo, Dietrich, Astaire and Mae West, and at its head was Hepburn. The fact that the female stars all played strong, independent roles, and that the most popular 'women' were Shirley Temple and Deanna Durbin, says much about 1930s film tastes. It was certainly too much for RKO who, after loyal support for their star through some bad years, cast her in a low-budget program-filler in the expectation that she would buy herself out of her contract – which she did.

Undaunted, Kate took herself and a long-cherished project off to Cukor. The screen rights for the Philip Barry comedy *Holiday*, in which she had understudied and screentested, were with Columbia, a minor studio who were delighted to make a one-off prestige picture with Cary Grant as the man who gets engaged to a wealthy girl, only to fall in love with Hepburn, playing the younger sister, and realize that some things are more important than money. The script was light and funny, the personalities worked, the setting was sumptuous and a familiar one to Kate, and the result was a delight. Cary Grant said at the time: 'As an actress she's a joy to work with. She's the most completely honest woman I've ever met.' But the theme had less impact in 1938, when Frank Capra's *You Can't Take it With You* had already won an Oscar, than when first aired in 1929, and again the film was a relative commercial failure. Hepburn said later: 'My career seemed to have ended with *Holiday*. I couldn't get a job for peanuts.' What made this worse was that she had tried hard for the lead in *Gone With the Wind*, with Cukor's support, but was passed over for an English unknown, Vivien Leigh.

Opposite: Hepburn and Tracy together for the first time in *Woman of the Year* (1942). When the project was first put to him, Tracy is supposed to have said: 'How can I do a picture with a woman who has dirt under her fingernails and who is of ambiguous sexuality and always wears pants?' After seeing *The Philadelphia Story,* he changed his mind.

Below: Another wedding scene, this time from *The Philadelphia Story.* The stuffy fiancé has fled, the reporter has offered for his 'golden girl, full of warmth and laughter and delight', but it is ex-husband Cary Grant who mops up the bride.

neur; her confidence in Barry's play was more than amply rewarded, since she made over $500,000 from the stage and screen rights to *The Philadelphia Story.*

In March 1939, when the play opened on Broadway after a successful provincial tour, however, the conclusion was not obvious, and rewriting continued right up until the last minute. Kate, remembering her destruction by the critics after the opening of *The Lake,* was awash with nerves and quite ready to believe the whole venture a disaster. But the critics thought otherwise: the *New York Post* found it 'difficult to take one's eyes off her,' while the *New York Times* recognized that she acted the part 'like a woman who has at last found the joy she has always been seeking in the theater.'

Initially Hollywood still played cautious, even after a triumphant post-Broadway tour lasting another 254 performances and grossing a cool $750,000. Then Louis B Mayer at MGM took a gamble and offered Hepburn a deal that gave her script approval and control of director and leading man. She enlisted Cukor, who added the prologue showing Tracy throwing her first husband and his golf clubs out through their front door, and Cary Grant, who demanded and got a hundred thousand

dollars and top billing. With James Stewart playing the idealistic reporter who also falls for the inimitable Miss Lord, the film was a natural. Interestingly, though, the Oscars went to Stewart and to the scriptwriter, and not to Kate. The Best Actress award went to Ginger Rogers, in the much inferior *Kitty Foyle,* and there were some who felt that this was the revenge of the 'little people of Hollywood.'

In a sense *The Philadelphia Story,* although it re-established Hepburn right at the top of the Hollywood tree, was the end rather than the beginning of an era. It was the last time she worked with Cary Grant, and it was perhaps the last example of a particular form of screwball comedy, with larger-than-life characters and well-heeled settings, before the advent of World War II rendered the genre obsolete. Hepburn's next project for MGM was very much a new beginning.

Various possibilities were aired before a new friend, Garson Kanin, showed Kate his script about the off-beat romance between a female political journalist and a tough sportswriter. Again doing her own wheeling and dealing, Kate showed this first to Joe Manckiewicz, her producer on *The Philadelphia Story,* and then to

Right: With co-star Robert Shayne in the Theater Guild production of *Without Love* (1942). The stage version went through considerable teething troubles but scriptwriter Donald Ogden Stewart tightened it up significantly when MGM decided to film it with Tracy as the male lead. *The New Yorker*, in fine acerbic style, wrote of the film: 'The somewhat metallic and stylized quality of Miss Hepburn's acting is almost perfectly suited to a role that is largely a vehicle for fashionable humor, and Mr Tracy's homespun behavior seems just about right for a man who really prefers airplanes to dames.'

Louis B Mayer. She wanted $100,000 for the authors, $100,000 for herself, and cast and director control; it is a measure of the confidence she inspired that Mayer agreed without a murmur. Kate wanted as her leading man an actor she had never met but much admired, Spencer Tracy. He had spent ten years in stock, marrying his leading lady Louise Treadwell in 1923. His big break had come in 1930, when he won the lead role in the prison drama *The Last Mile* and then co-starred with Bogart in the film version. By 1935 he was a major star, but was also known as having a major drink problem and could miss hours or even days of shooting. Despite this he was immensely respected for his understated acting technique: 'Any actor who's ever played a scene with Spencer will tell you,' said Clark Gable (whom Tracy in turn called 'the King'), 'There's nothing like it. He mesmerizes you. Those eyes of his – and what goes on behind them. Nobody's better than when they act with him.'

Tracy accepted the part in what by now was called *Woman of the Year* but was less impressed with Hepburn's reputation than she with his. The story goes that when they met she said 'I'm afraid I am a little tall for you, Mr Tracy' – at five foot ten in her heels she was only an inch shorter than him. 'Don't worry, Miss Hepburn,' he replied. 'I'll soon cut you down to my size.' Which of course is just what their on-screen partnership was about, and it was a conscious decision on the part of Kate and her advisers that this should be so. It had become

clear that there was no film future for her as a loner – she needed a film partnership to further and develop her career. To modern audiences there is something unattractive, even disturbing, in the metamorphosis of the arrogant, independent Hepburn of the 1930s social comedies into a fighter prepared and needing to be tamed by a man. In *Woman of the Year* the unlikely couple marry but Tess Harding (Kate) sees no reason to change her lifestyle or shoulder any domestic burdens, and on the evening that she is named Woman of the Year her husband walks out. Initially the ending was left ambiguous, but in the course of shooting it was changed to leave Kate firmly in the kitchen, making a mess of the breakfast.

Here at last was a performance that conformed to a recognizable stereotype and critics welcomed it. According to *Time:* 'As a lady columnist she is just right; as a working reporter he is practically perfect. For once strident Katharine Hepburn is properly subdued.' It was also plain to all those on set that the two stars had simply and sincerely fallen in love in the course of shooting. Until then Kate had perhaps been too much involved in establishing and re-establishing herself in the movie world, too well supported by her family and small circle of close friends, to feel the need of a more than transitory relationship. In an interview recorded early in 1991 to mark the publication of her autobiography, she firmly states her view that women's position in the world is so much less advantageous than men's that 'it makes me want to choke most of the men I know.' But by the time she met Tracy she had come to terms with her own abilities, finally felt secure in her chosen career and, as she memorably says, 'was in a position to be adorable to someone else.' She also recognized at once that she could be deeply useful. Half-way through making *Woman of the Year* Tracy vanished. He was finally found by Kate in a bar, brought home, sobered up and covered for, and so began a thirty-year relationship; one that did not at all reflect their on-screen relationship. In the films it is Tracy who is the strong, quiet, dominant partner and Hepburn who in the end succumbs; off-screen it was she who provided the solidarity and continuity, he who sometimes rebeled or wavered. Although the film partnership with Tracy certainly gave Hepburn's career an essential fillip – and the private relationship clearly brought her immense joy for many years – it is arguable that it actually came to hold back her development as an actress. The next real stage in her career does not begin until the making of *The African Queen* in 1951.

In 1942, however, after a brief pause while Kate returned to the stage to tour in another Philip Barry comedy, *Without Love*, which proved unready for Broadway, MGM reunited their clearly successful team in *Keeper of the Flame*. Although directed by Cukor, this proved a waxwork affair, the uncovering of a great man's Fascist past, and was the last time that the 35-year-old Hepburn was to play a straight glamour role. It also showed Kate playing second fiddle to Tracy, in another clear reversal of their private lives. Her own tastes ran to much more challenging material, and she put all her considerable energy into trying to persuade MGM to do a screen version of Eugene O'Neill's play *Mourning Becomes Electra*, his classic reinterpretation of the *Oresteia* set in the aftermath of the Civil War. MGM found the project too sexually provocative, however, and Kate made an impressive on-the-record press protest at the meretricious standards this decision implied. Her screen role with Tracy might require her to be submissive but the real Kate was a mature and increasingly formidable woman.

Her next movie venture, while Tracy made *A Guy Named Joe* and *The Seventh Cross*, was a real oddity, *Dragon Seed*, based on a Pearl Buck novel about the Chinese peasants' long struggle against Japanese aggression. As soon as both she and Tracy were free, MGM cast them in the film version of *Without Love*, which

Below: *Keeper of the Flame* (1942) was the second film to feature Hepburn and Tracy as co-stars, in a strongly anti-Fascist but not wholly successful piece. It was directed by George Cukor, who tried to achieve the moody suspense technique of which Hitchcock was the acknowledged master.

and Tracy himself were both keen, and shooting started immediately on their return.

Adam's Rib is a battle-of-the-sexes comedy about a couple, both lawyers, who find themselves respectively defending (Hepburn) and prosecuting (Tracy) a woman who has shot and injured her husband after tracking him through the streets of New York to the lovenest where he is two-timing her. The tensions of the trial and the women's rights issues it raises spill over into the marriage, and the Gordon/Kanin partnership provided the Hepburn/Tracy team with some aggressively trueto-life dialogue even if, as ever, the story ends with capitulation by Hepburn. The movie was shot on location in New York, which made a pleasant change from tired Hollywood sets and even tireder Hollywood extras, and had a rather dour theme song by Cole Porter to give it an air of raffish respectability. The result was a resounding success, which sent the sagging box-office ratings of both stars soaring again, and at the time was regarded as the best of all their joint ventures. Bosley Crowther in *The New York Times* saw Hepburn and Tracy as:

The stellar performers in this show, and their perfect compatibility in comic capers is delightful to see. A line thrown away, a lifted eyebrow, a smile or a sharp, resounding slap on a tender part of the anatomy is as natural as breathing to them.

Off screen the partnership did not run so smoothly. Tracy was not an easy man, unsociable at the best of times – as was Hepburn – and never more so than when he was engaged on one of his periodic drinking bouts. He be-

came hostile to Kate's support, which he saw as interference, and resentful of any suggestion that he should seek professional help. By the time he had made *Malaya*, his next film, they were virtually estranged. To add to Hepburn's difficulties, the House UnAmerican Activities Committee was set on cleaning up the film industry, and on June 8th, 1949, published a long list of film people who were condemned as 'Communist appeasers.' Kate's name appeared on this along with that of Pearl Buck (presumably for writing a book on China) and Maurice Chevalier (considered a died-in-thewool reactionary in Europe).

It was a good moment for a change. Shooting *Adam's Rib* in New York had reminded Kate of the joys of Broadway, and she finally acquiesced in a long-planned Theater Guild project to put on Shakespeare's *As You Like It* with herself as Rosalind, the duke's daughter who is banished to the greenwood and disguises herself as a boy. Her initial reluctance was as much to do with the failure of her crossdressing role in *Sylvia Scarlett* as with alarm at playing Shakespeare. Her old friend Constance Collier, a fine Shakespearean in her own right, agreed to coach Kate; Shakespeare required a far greater range and color of voice than had been needed for any of the modern roles Kate had played on stage, as well as the ability to speak the verse with meaning.

Kate at 43 was an elegant, supremely fit woman, in a mold that might be more recognizable today than in the more indolent 1940s. Her voice had deepened, perhaps not unconnected with her heavy smoking, so that

Right: Hepburn with Tracy in *Adam's Rib* (1949), in which both played lawyers. As *Newsweek* described the movie: 'Here again is the famous battle of the sexes, strictly without benefit of August Strindberg and waged in the home and courtroom shared by Adam Bonner (Tracy) and his wife Amanda (Hepburn). Although both are lawyers and given to calling each other Pinky in their kittenish moments, there is no confusing their respective pronouncements on a woman's right to take a few compulsive potshots at a philandering husband.'

Left: With William Prince playing Orlando in the 1950 Broadway production of *As You Like It*. Although the production was an immense hit with audiences, the critics were less happy with her portrayal of Rosalind as a shy and limpid girl. As *The New York Times* put it: 'She is not a helpless, bewitched, moon-struck maiden swooning through a magic forest. . . Miss Hepburn has too sharply defined a personality for such romantic make-believe. . . And is this a New England accent we hear twanging the strings of Shakespeare's lyre?'

Below: A relaxed and candid moment from *Adam's Rib*.

the harshness that had drawn critical comment had mellowed. She had learned a greater confidence in her own acting abilities from Tracy, who was always described as a natural, and her knowledge of both stage and film technique was vast. The pre-Broadway tour of *As You Like It* was an immense success, and the play ran for 180 performances on Broadway. The public was fascinated by the thought of a famous screenstar on stage, although the critics were slightly less enraptured: 'Miss Hepburn's legs are always poetry,' said one unkindly, 'But I cannot help feeling that she mistakes the Forest of Arden for the campus of Bryn Mawr.' It was Kate's decision to play Rosalind not as a managing young woman, as might perhaps have come more convincingly from someone with her reputation and manner, but as a shy and restrained girl. Broadway was followed by a midwest tour, but meanwhile Tracy was anxious for a reunion and promised to stop drinking. He was then kept busy by MGM on *Father of the Bride* and *Father's Little Dividend,* keeping him committed to California until well into 1951. Kate was desperate for a script that would return her to Hollywood to be with him, but she was no longer seen as eligible for parts requiring either youth or glamour and there was precious little in the way of interesting parts for middle-aged women – a fact that still holds true today. To make things worse, the growth of television was threatening the movie world, which had to shoot bigger and better, more real and more exotic, to compete with this dangerous sibling.

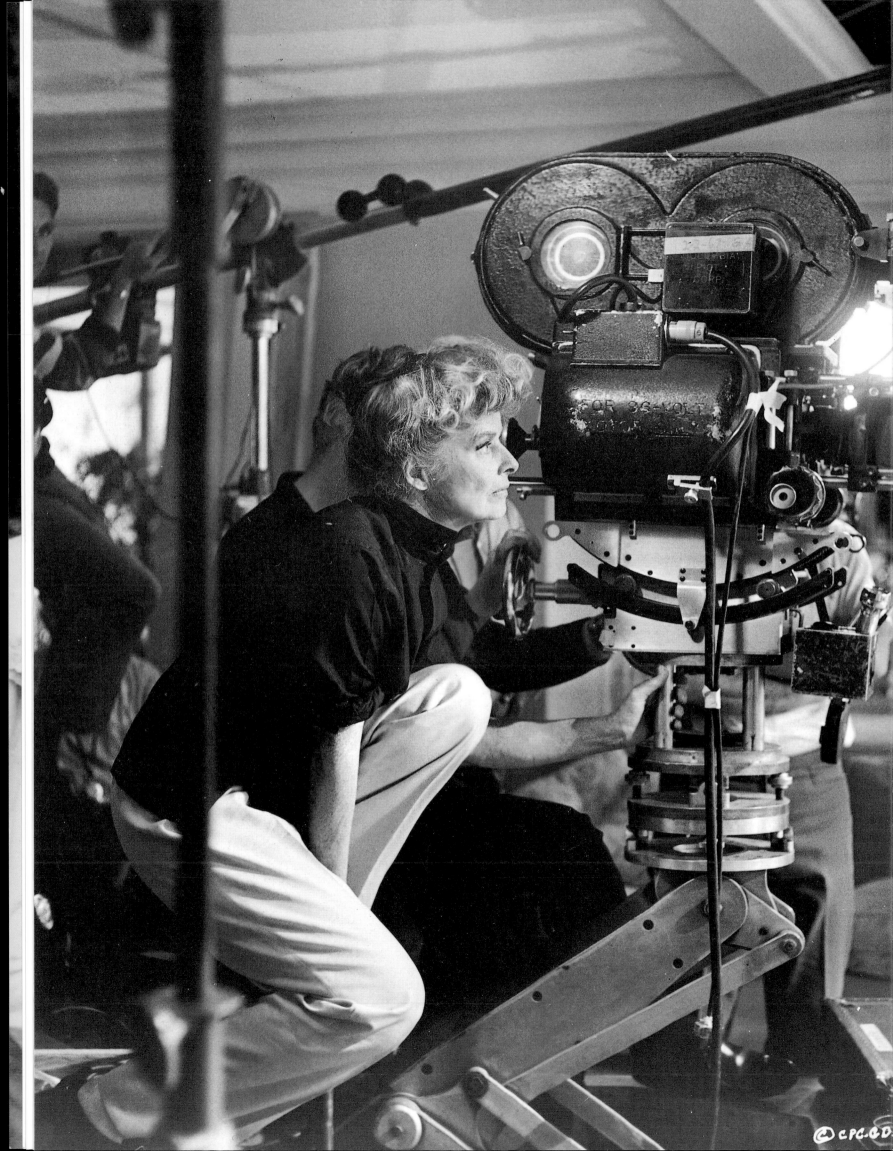

to say that I am a beauty with a well-proportioned face. But when I was beginning they thought I was just a freak with a lot of freckles.'

Regrettably her next release was a much less successful movie, both critically and commercially. *The Madwoman of Chaillot,* the film version of a classic play by Jean Giraudoux, is the story of an eccentric countess who plans to save Paris from a group of war-minded capitalists who want to turn it into a giant oilfield. The director should have been John Huston,

with whom Kate had worked on *The African Queen,* but he opted out two weeks before filming began and Bryan Forbes failed to rescue the resulting muddle, despite an amazingly starry cast.

Before she had left for Europe to work on these two costume dramas, Kate's old friend Irene Selznick had persuaded her to audition for the role of the ageless couturière Coco Chanel, in a musical written by Alan Jay Lerner (of My *Fair Lady* fame) and André Previn. At first Kate laughed uproariously at the

Above: With O'Toole as Henry II in one of their more amicable moments during *The Lion in Winter.* Their mutual respect and affection is no match for their political ambitions.

Opposite: Perfectionist to the last, Kate checks a camera angle on the set of *Guess Who's Coming to Dinner* (1967), her last film with Tracy.

thought of singing in public then, as ever, she rose to the challenge, took singing lessons, and landed the part. Chanel herself approved the choice, and Kate recognized a lot of herself in the 86-year-old Parisian:

We're two females who have never been intimidated by the world, who have never shifted our styles to conform to public opinion . . . her capacity for survival is what really fascinates me.

So, at the age of 62, she committed herself to the punishing Broadway schedule of eight performances a week.

The idea of casting Kate as Coco was a stroke of genius but the musical, with immensely complicated sets by Cecil Beaton, precious little plot and an undistinguished score by Previn, was a dinosaur of a piece at a time when the old-fashioned spectacular Broadway musical seemed an anomaly. Reviewers were unimpressed but, as *The New York Times* observed: 'The show has become a showcase, a form of endearment, a gesture of assent, an open palm of respect.' Regardless of reviews, Kate on Broadway proved capable of packing the theater every night for six months, an achievement she was to match twice more

in the next decade. After shunning publicity and adulation for nearly four decades, she had become a massively popular cult figure – and found that she liked it, that it helped to fill the gaping hole left by the deaths of her father and of Tracy, the two fundamental male influences in her life.

Her first movie of the early 1970s was less successful; it was the usual problem of finding the right script. The film version of Euripides' *The Trojan Women*, with Vanessa Redgrave, Irene Papas and Genevieve Bujold, failed to rise above the staginess of the screenplay and the very disparate accents of the four principals, but as Kate said: 'I've never done Greek tragedy and before my time runs out I'd like to have tried everything.' She also longed to make another film in Hollywood, and all seemed set fair for a film version of Graham Greene's *Travels with My Aunt* – until MGM decided that they did not like the version of the script with which Kate had become closely identified, and wanted to show the character as a younger woman in flashback. So once again, for the last time in her life, and immediately after winning two successive Oscars, Kate Hepburn was fired from a movie.

Above: With Nanette Newman in *The Madwoman of Chaillot* (1969), a tame follow-up to *The Lion in Winter*. The decision to update Giraudoux's timeless fantasy of a play displeased John Huston, the original director, and gave an earth-bound heaviness to what should have been a lightweight whimsy.

Opposite: Despite her continued vitality and glowing good looks, Kate became sensitive in her later years about the crepiness of her neck, and from the 1960s on was invariably shrouded up to the chin.

Above: *Coco* was something of an anachronism as a musical, but it played to packed houses. Here Coco (Hepburn) chronicles her early career for a young model (Gale Dixon) whom she has taken under her wing.

Right: *Rooster Cogburn* was an attempt to recapture some of the atmosphere of both *The African Queen* and John Wayne's Oscar-winning role in *True Grit*. One reviewer summed up the prevailing reaction when he wrote: 'The plot is negligible, the direction minimal, but the two Powerhouses carry it through entertainingly. Who could ask for more?'

Opposite: Hepburn in Wales in 1978 for the making of the television play *The Corn is Green.*

Instead, after *The Trojan Women*, she made a number of television films, a new medium for her but a quick and economical way of making a permanent record of a classic play. The first of these was Edward Albee's *A Delicate Balance* (1973), directed by Tony Richardson and co-starring Paul Scofield, to be followed by Tennessee Williams' *A Glass Menagerie.* In 1975 she returned to London to make *Love Among the Ruins,* a delightful Edwardian love story between a former Shakespearean actress and the famous barrister with whom she once had a forgotten affair; the barrister was played by her old friend Laurence Olivier, the first time they had acted together. Another old friend, George Cukor, directed, and it was with him that Kate again returned to the UK in 1979 to make *The Corn is Green,* Emlyn Williams's story of an English teacher in a Welsh mining village.

Her only major Hollywood movie of the 1970s, *Rooster Cogburn,* co-starred another craggy survivor, though in a rather different mold – John Wayne. The film was dismissed as a poor follow-up to *The African Queen* and *True Grit* and memorably panned by the *New Yorker* as 'just a belch from the Nixon era.' But

the two stars, despite their fundamentally different political viewpoints, developed a healthy respect for each other and a good rapport, and commercially the movie was a hit. Another Broadway venture, *A Matter of Gravity*, co-starring a pre-Superman Christopher Reeve, again brought the audiences streaming in, despite the slightness of the play, as did *West Side Waltz* in 1981. Hepburn had concluded that there was a lot more potential in being an old stage actress than an old screen actress.

She could, however, be lured back on screen by the right project. *Olly Olly Oxen Free* (1979), a delicious, absurd film about an eccentric junkyard proprietress who accidentally goes hot-air ballooning with two children she has befriended, was hampered by a leaden script but 'they let me play most of it up in a balloon and how often do you get to do that at 70?' In 1985 she made *The Ultimate Solution of Grace Quigley*, an extremely black comedy about an elderly woman's flourishing euthanasia business. But the late film for which she will always be best and most fondly remembered is, of course, *On Golden Pond*.

On Golden Pond, a play by Ernest Thompson, had had a reasonably successful run first off and then on Broadway in 1978. It is the story of a couple, married 50 years, who come to spend the summer in their cottage on Golden Pond in Maine. Norman has a heart condition and his wife Ethel, ten years his junior, is battling to keep him alive and happy – an uphill task given his disposition, and

Above: Two giants of the screen together at last in *On Golden Pond* (1981); both won Oscars for their roles, although Hepburn's was more a sentimental tribute to her career as a whole than an award for this particular part, which was anyway less substantial than Fonda's and which she unselfishly ensured did not compete.

Right: With Jane Fonda, who plays her father's daughter.

Opposite: Hepburn continues to live contentedly in the same New York brownstone that she bought soon after her marriage, surrounded by devoted friends and family.

Left: 'I'm a romantic painter of landscapes and people. I've always been more interested in what painters have to say – because painting interests me more than acting. You do it by yourself, you don't say somebody else's lines.'

further complicated by the arrival of their divorced daughter, determined to thrash out her relationship with her father before he dies, plus her appalling lover and his difficult 13-year-old son. A sentimental piece, this would probably never have made it on to film, had Jane Fonda not seen it as a vehicle for her dying father to make his public farewell. She acquired the screen rights and put up her own salary as insurance for her father, just as Hepburn had done for Tracy 14 years earlier. Given the background the part of Ethel was irresistible to Hepburn even though, as with her films with Tracy, the male lead was the key to the story. Extraordinarily she and Henry Fonda had never met. On the first day of shooting she gave him Tracy's favorite hat, and he wore it throughout the film.

The result is film history. The background to the movie was common knowledge and this, plus impeccable if tear-struck acting, lift a waffling, potentially forgettable play (described by one acerbic critic as a 'hunk of sub-Chekhovian New England marshmallow') into the realms of mythology. *On Golden Pond* articulated for 1980s audiences a growing disenchantment with the violent, high-tech movies which dominated the box offices, and a renewed desire for the old-fashioned values of warmth and humanity which Hollywood had once been so adept at expressing. Middle-aged filmgoers returned to the cinemas in droves and the film became the runaway hit of the season. *Newsweek*'s review reflected the almost unanimously favorable critical judgment:

The story is sentimental. But call it what you may – middlebrow, manipulative – the movie lives and breathes and has the power to pluck a responsive chord in all but the most cynical viewer . . . Hepburn is radiant and physically astonishing, whether swinging from the arms of a chair or diving from a boat . . . an intelligent tearjerker, a handcrafted heartbreaker.

It was Fonda who received the lion's share of the accolades at the time; some critics thought that Hepburn's performance was over-sentimentalized. She was also handicapped by an eye condition which made her look permanently weepy (a legacy of her famous fall into a polluted Venetian canal for *Summertime*) and the onset of Parkinson's disease, which gave her the shakes. Fonda's Academy Award was widely predicted but when Hepburn too carried off an Oscar, breaking her own record, it created a sensation.

In 1984 a survey of 4,500 American teenagers asked who they would name as their ten contemporary heroes. The only woman on the list, which included such names as Michael Jackson and Clint Eastwood, was Katharine Hepburn, at number seven one ahead of the Pope. She was 77 at the time. Once asked if she had ever planned to retire, she replied: 'In a lifetime of gardening, I have never yet seen a laurel on which one could rest really comfortably. There are no laurels in my life, just new challenges.'

Opposite: As the warm-hearted and inspiring teacher Miss Moffat in a television version of Emlyn Williams's play *The Corn is Green*, which also starred Anna Massey, Toyah Wilcox and Patricia Hayes, and was directed by one of Kate's oldest friends, George Cukor.

1968
The Lion in Winter, DIR. Anthony Harvey, co-starring Peter O'Toole, Jane Merrow, John Castle, Timothy Dalton, Anthony Hopkins

1969
The Madwoman of Chaillot, DIR. Bryan Forbes, co-starring Charles Boyer, Edith Evans, Margaret Leighton, Nanette Newman, Richard Chamberlain, Yul Brynner, Donald Pleasance, Danny Kaye

1971
The Trojan Women, DIR. Michael Cacoyannis, co-starring Vanessa Redgrave, Genevieve Bujold, Irene Papas

1973
A Delicate Balance, DIR. Tony Richardson, co-starring Paul Scofield, Lee Remick

1975
Rooster Cogburn, DIR. Stuart Miller, co-starring John Wayne

1978
Olly Olly Oxen Free, DIR. Richard Colla, co-starring Kevin McKenzie

1981
On Golden Pond, DIR. Mark Rydell, co-starring Henry Fonda, Jane Fonda

Above: A color portrait taken at about the time she met Tracy.

1967
Guess Who's Coming to Dinner, DIR. Stanley Kramer, co-starring Spencer Tracy, Sidney Poitier, Katharine Houghton

1985
The Ultimate Solution of Grace Quigley, DIR. Anthony Harvey, co-starring Nick Nolte

Right: Cukor directing Kate and Sir Laurence Olivier in the television film *Love Among the Ruins* (1975), the delightful story of the reunion in old age of a pair of lovers. As *Variety* noted: 'The three together have more show business experience than the Atlantic has water. The professionalism showed through.'

Index

Figures in *italics* refer to illustrations

SPACE GUIDES

EXPLORING THE EARTH

PETER GREGO

QED Publishing

Copyright © QED Publishing 2007

First published in the UK in 2007 by
QED Publishing
A Quarto Group company
226 City Road
London EC1V 2TT
www.qed-publishing.co.uk

A catalogue record for this book is available from the British Library.

ISBN 978-1-84538-684-9

Written by Peter Grego
Produced by Calcium
Editor Sarah Eason
Illustrations by Geoff Ward
Picture Researcher Maria Joannou

Publisher Steve Evans
Creative Director Zeta Davies
Senior Editor Hannah Ray

Printed and bound in China

Picture credits
Key: T = top, B = bottom, C = centre, L = left, R = right, FC = front cover, BC = back cover

Corbis/Bettmann 16, /Tom Bean 24–25, /Jonathan Blair 22–23, /Ric Ergenbright 26–27, /David Muench 23B; **ESA**/NASA and G. Bacon 6; **Getty Images**/Iconica FCB, 11B, /Imagebank 20–21, /Photodisc FCT, 4, BC, /Taxi 16–17; **NASA** 9B, 10, 18, 19B, /GSFC 1, 19T, /GSFC/Jacques Descloitres/MODIS Rapid Response Team 12–13, /GSFC/Craig Mayhew and Robert Simmon 28–29, /IKONOS 3, /JPL-Caltech 7T, 7B, 8, /USGS 14, 15T; **NGDC** 29; **NOAA** 27, 28, /Lieutenant Philip Hall 13; **Science Photo Library**/Chris Butler 26, /Mark Garlick 5T, /David A Hardy 9T, /Walter Pacholka/Astropics 11T, / Soames Summerhays FCC, /Dirk Wiersma 23T; **USGS** 24, 25, /Seth Moran 21

Words in **bold** can be found in the Glossary on pages 30–31.

Contents

The blue planet

Our **planet**, the Earth, is one of eight planets that make up our **Solar System**. They circle a star called the **Sun**. We depend upon the Sun's tremendous heat and light to create our weather and help keep us, other animals and plants alive.

The Earth is a medium-sized planet, the fifth largest in the Solar System. It measures 12 756km in diameter, so it would take you several years to walk around it.

Our place in the Universe

Earth is our home in the vast **Universe**. Since the first astronaut blasted off into **space**, in April 1961, fewer than 1000 people have managed to see our planet from space. There, it appears a beautiful, blue globe spinning through the inky black vastness of space. It is an overwhelming sight.

Our planet, the Earth, photographed by 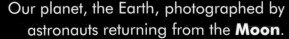 astronauts returning from the **Moon**.

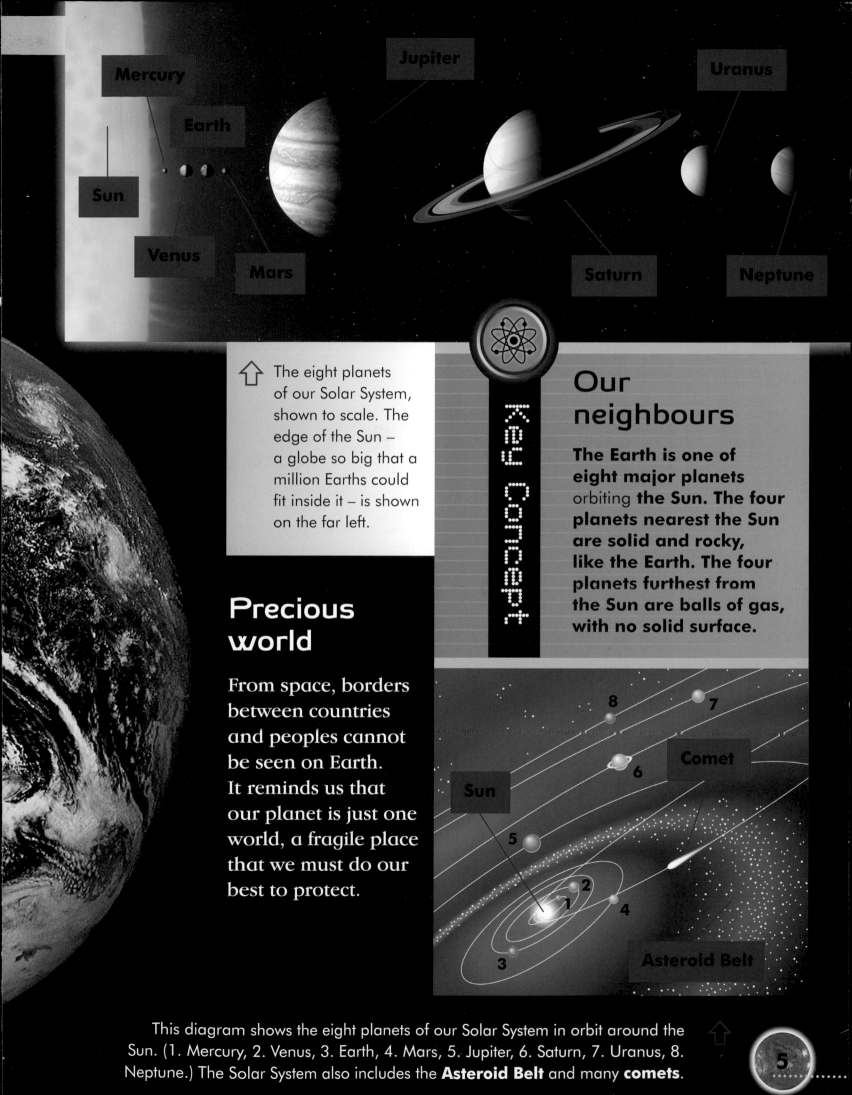

Mercury

Earth

Sun

Venus

Mars

Jupiter

Saturn

Uranus

Neptune

⬆ The eight planets of our Solar System, shown to scale. The edge of the Sun – a globe so big that a million Earths could fit inside it – is shown on the far left.

Our neighbours

The Earth is one of eight major planets orbiting **the Sun. The four planets nearest the Sun are solid and rocky, like the Earth. The four planets furthest from the Sun are balls of gas, with no solid surface.**

Precious world

From space, borders between countries and peoples cannot be seen on Earth. It reminds us that our planet is just one world, a fragile place that we must do our best to protect.

Sun

8

7

Comet

6

5

1

2

4

3

Asteroid Belt

This diagram shows the eight planets of our Solar System in orbit around the Sun. (1. Mercury, 2. Venus, 3. Earth, 4. Mars, 5. Jupiter, 6. Saturn, 7. Uranus, 8. Neptune.) The Solar System also includes the **Asteroid Belt** and many **comets**.

Birth of the Solar System

More than 4.6 billion years ago, the blast from an exploding star disturbed a nearby cloud of dust and gas. The blast pushed parts of the cloud together, which made them denser (thicker and bulkier). These areas had more **gravity** – a force that pulls little objects towards bigger objects. Gravity made the denser parts of the cloud gather together into more solid shapes. Scientists think this is how the material that makes up the Sun was first gathered together.

A star is born

As the dust cloud became heavier, it began to spin. This produced a flattened disk of dust and gas, which spun around the denser material at its centre. As the centre contracted, it became even thicker and hotter. Eventually, the centre became so hot that it began to burn. It became a star – the newborn Sun had begun to shine.

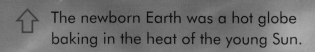 The newborn Earth was a hot globe baking in the heat of the young Sun.

The young Solar System

Meanwhile, parts of the disk of dust and gas surrounding the Sun were also drawn together by gravity. This produced some large planets, lots of moons, and thousands of rocky **asteroids** and icy comets. All of these objects made up the young Solar System.

Powerful winds from the new Sun blew away all the light gases in the inner Solar System. Only objects made out of heavier materials remained. Our Earth was one of these objects.

⇧ The young Sun was surrounded by clouds of dust and gas, which clumped together to create the planets.

The gravity of the ⇨ young planets swept up any rock and dust that orbited them, but larger chunks of rocks remained further out in the solar system. These made up the Asteroid Belt between Mars and Jupiter.

Ancient zircon

Crystals taken from rocks in Australia were found to be 4.4 billion years old. They formed just after the Earth was created.

7

The young Earth

As asteroids smashed into its surface, the young Earth's temperature rose. It's gravity kept pulling in more material and, as the Earth grew bigger, its inside continued to get hotter and hotter. It soon became hot enough to melt the metals in its rocks. These **molten** metals sank to the Earth's centre and formed its **core**. Lighter material rose to form the planet's outer layer, called its crust. Between the core and the crust is a layer of very hot molten rock, called the **mantle**.

The Moon is thought to have been formed when a planet the size of Mars crashed into the Earth.

Amazing

A big whack

The Moon was formed by a crash. Scientists believe that a planet half the size of ours struck the young Earth, throwing out a massive sheet of melted material. Much of this material was pulled back together by gravity, and formed the Moon.

Asteroid attack

For more than a billion years after the Earth was formed, asteroids frequently smashed through its thin, rocky crust. This allowed hot, melted rock to burst through and spread over the surface as sheets of bubbling **lava**. Over time, these helped to build up the Earth's crust.

The Moon was also hit by asteroids, which formed **craters** on its surface. If the Earth's surface hadn't continued to be changed by the movements of its crust, **volcanoes** and **weathering**, it would have as many craters as the Moon.

Both the Earth and the Moon were hit by asteroids in their early history.

Lakes and seas

Once asteroids started hitting the planet less often, the Earth's crust began to cool and thicken. Volcanoes continued to erupt, spewing out lava and releasing water vapour into the air. As the Earth cooled, water vapour turned into liquid. Small puddles slowly turned into lakes and seas. Icy comets sometimes hit the Earth, too, adding to the water on its surface when they melted. The Earth now had areas of land and of water.

We can see craters billions of years old on the surface of the Moon. Despite being very old, they look quite new. They have steep walls and sharp rims, and large mountains often rise from their centres.

Continents, plates and mountains

AAll the landmasses (**continents**) seen on Earth today were once joined together in a single, giant landmass known as Pangaea, which was surrounded by a huge ocean. However, the molten rock of the mantle pushed up on the Earth's crust, causing it to break up into smaller pieces, called **plates**. And as the crust broke into plates, Pangaea was split into smaller pieces, too.

Shifting plates

Gaps between the plates became wider as molten **magma** from the mantle pushed into them. This made South America break away from Africa, and India and Australia break away from Antarctica. A hundred million years ago, molten magma also separated Europe from North America. Ocean water filled the space between these new continents, creating new seas and oceans.

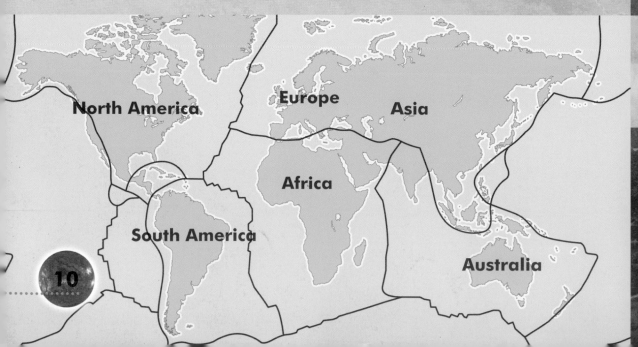

The red lines show the plates that make up the Earth's crust.

North America

Europe

Asia

Africa

South America

Australia

Alfred Wegener (1880–1930)

We know that the plates of the Earth are moving, and that the Earth used to look very different. But how did we find this out? By looking at the shapes of the continents, we can see that they would once have fitted together, like a giant jigsaw. For instance, if the west coast of Africa was placed next to the east coast of South America, they would fit snugly together. Their rocks and fossils are also similar, suggesting they were once one landmass. The theory that continents move, or drift, was first suggested by German scientist Alfred Wegener, only 100 years ago. Although they move by just a few centimetres each year, over millions of years this adds up to a great distance. We call this moving of continents continental drift.

⬆ The Himalayas is the Earth's biggest mountain range – and it's still growing. It was created when India pushed into southern Asia, forcing up the Earth's crust.

⬆ Mountains are one of the results of plate movement.

Mountains

Mountains are formed when two plates push against each other, forcing up Earth's crust. Sometimes the crust beneath an ocean pushes against the crust beneath a continent. When this happens, the crust beneath the continent is pushed up to make a mountain. The biggest mountain ranges, however, occur when the plates beneath two continents collide and both crumple up.

Earth changes

If the Earth could have been seen from space 100 years ago, the shapes and positions of the main areas of land would look the same as those seen today. However, the Earth's surface is constantly changing. Some changes happen quickly, such as those caused by earthquakes and volcanoes. Others happen over a longer period of time, such as the wearing away of rocks by weather and water, or continental drift.

Parts of Earth's surface are ⇨ built up when material gathers over a long period of time. This is called sedimentation. The small islands at the mouth of the River Lena, in Russia, were formed in this way. They were made when mud, small bits of rock and other loose material flowed downstream and collected where the river meets the sea. The islands break up the river into a network of smaller channels, called a delta.

Land shifts

We humans have only been recording our planet for a few thousand years. This is an incredibly short time compared to the life of the Earth. The Earth is about 4.6 billion years old. If we could hop into a time machine and zoom through the history of the Earth so fast that each century passed in one second, we would be amazed to see mountains being built and wearing away, spaces for oceans being made or squeezed out of existence, coastlines being created and destroyed, and new continents being formed. At the same time, the sea level would rise and fall over time, as the **ice caps** at the north and south poles grew or shrank.

Key concept

Continental drift

Powered by deep movements within the Earth's hot mantle, continental drift is still happening. The Atlantic Ocean is widening by about 4cm each year. India is continuing to collide with south Asia, crumpling the solid crust between the two continents. This is forcing up the mighty Himalayan Mountains even further.

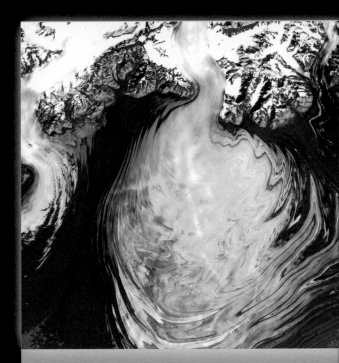

⇧ This glacier (part of an ice cap) is slowly melting, as the Earth's **climate** warms up. In a few hundred years' time the ice may have melted completely. If many glaciers melt, sea levels will rise and flood large areas of land. Earth will look different once again.

⇦ This map shows how Europe might look if the sea level rises by 100m. The lighter blue areas show land that would be flooded.

North Sea

Baltic Sea

Atlantic Ocean

Black Sea

Mediterranean Sea

Volcanoes and earthquakes

Volcanoes are formed in places where hot, molten rock breaks through the Earth's crust and onto the surface. Like mountains, volcanoes are usually found where plates collide or move apart. There are about 1000 active volcanoes around the world. No two volcanoes are exactly alike. Volcanoes around the edges of continents are often tall and steep-sided, built up over the years by eruptions of thick, slow-moving lava and piles of ash.

Vesuvius

One of the most famous volcanoes is Vesuvius, on the west coast of Italy. Vesuvius began as a small, volcanic hill about 25 000 years ago, and it is now 1300m high. Almost 2000 years ago, an eruption of Vesuvius destroyed the nearby Roman towns of Pompeii and Herculaneum.

In 79CE, the ancient Roman towns of Pompeii and Herculaneum were completely buried beneath volcanic ash and rock when the volcano Vesuvius erupted. The bodies of victims (like those shown here) were preserved in layers of volcanic ash and can still be seen today.

This is Mount St Helens. A mighty mountain peak used to be where the gaping crater is now.

Amazing

Mount St Helens

One of the most devastating eruptions of recent times happened in May 1980 in Washington State, north-western USA, when Mount St Helens blew its top. The immense explosion blasted a column of ash into the air up to 25km high.

Earthquakes

Earthquakes happen when two plates are pushed together and suddenly slide past each other for a short distance.

Earthquakes range from mild vibrations to devastating shakings of the ground, which can topple buildings. Small earthquakes happen in Britain each year, but few cause any real damage. Large buildings in areas that suffer from large earthquakes, such as California and Japan, are built to withstand the violent jolting of the ground. Buildings in poorer countries may not be so well made, and great loss of life can occur when an earthquake happens near a big city in which many people live.

Asia

North America

Pacific Ocean

South America

Australia

☐ **Ring of Fire**

Earthquakes are common in an area known as the Pacific Ring of Fire. Here, the plate beneath the ocean is being pushed beneath the surrounding continental plates.

Inside the Earth

The Earth's natural movements have revealed a lot about the rocks that lie beneath its surface. Layers of rock that were once buried have been lifted up as the crust has moved and shifted. When the Grand Canyon formed, in Arizona in the USA, it made a cut in the Earth's crust 1600m deep, uncovering rocks that are more than a billion years old!

Drilling into Earth

Scientists have also been able to learn more about Earth's rocks by drilling into its crust. The USA launched one of the first big scientific drilling projects in 1957. It was called Project Mohole. It drilled through the ocean floor off the coast of Mexico, cutting into the sea bed 3.5km below the water's surface. The project dug up rocks over five million years old.

Earth

Moon

⬆ Comparing the interiors of the Earth and the Moon. The Earth's insides are hot and molten, while the Moon is much cooler and solid.

Digging deep

The Kola Superdeep Borehole project in northern Russia has drilled down more than 12km, and brought up rock samples more than 2.7 billion years old.

Amazing

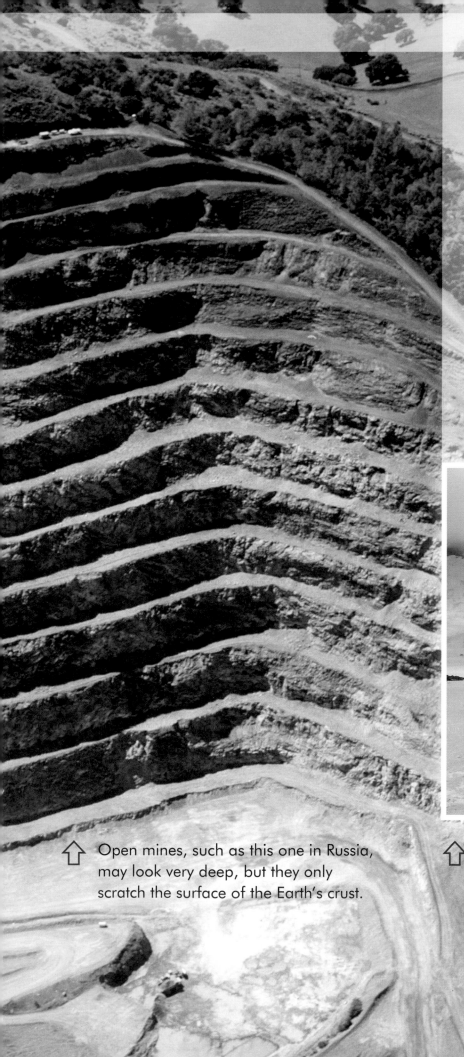

Measuring shakes

Incredibly, scientists have learned about the thickness and **density** of the Earth's crust, mantle and core by studying the shaking movements caused by earthquakes. Earthquakes cause different kinds of shaking motion – some push and pull the crust, others move it up and down. By measuring these motions, scientists can tell how dense the material is beneath the crust, and so build up a picture of inside our planet.

⬆ Open mines, such as this one in Russia, may look very deep, but they only scratch the surface of the Earth's crust.

⬆ A scientific station has been set up on Mount St Helens to measure earthquakes and earth movements.

17

Rocks

Three main types of rock make up the Earth: igneous rock, sedimentary rock and metamorphic rock.

Igneous rocks

Igneous rocks are formed when molten rock cools and hardens. The igneous rocks formed on the Earth's surface are called volcanic rocks. Basalt is a volcanic rock. Pumice is also a volcanic rock, which cooled as it was blasted out of a volcano. It is rough and full of holes caused by the gas bubbles that frothed in it when it was molten.

Igneous rocks formed beneath the Earth's surface are called plutonic rocks. They cooled down more slowly than volcanic rocks. Granite is a type of plutonic rock.

Rock hunting

Project

Collect local rock samples and try to identify them. Your local library or museum may have information on the types of rock in your area. Perhaps you are living on an ancient volcano, or on ground that used to be part of the sea bed!

⇧ Granite is a plutonic igneous rock, made when molten magma cools deep below the ground. It is extremely hard.

This is a sedimentary rock called a conglomerate, because it is made up of lots of rock fragments cemented together with a finer material.

Sedimentary rocks

These are the most common type of rock. Sedimentary rocks, such as sandstone, are formed by the breaking down and weathering of other rocks. Material settling on a sea bed can also harden over time to become a sedimentary rock, such as limestone or chalk. These sedimentary rocks are made up of the skeletons of tiny sea creatures. Coal is a sedimentary rock formed from the remains of dead trees and plants.

Metamorphic rocks

Metamorphic rocks are made when one type of rock is changed into a different type by extreme heat and pressure within the Earth's crust (called compression). Igneous and sedimentary rocks can be changed into metamorphic rocks, and existing metamorphic rocks can be changed into different metamorphic rocks.

Gneiss (say 'neece') is a type of metamorphic rock.

Earth ages

A hundred years ago, geologists studying the Earth knew that most rocks must be extremely old. For example, a rock such as coal – made from ancient trees and the remains of other plants – needs countless thousands of years of compression beneath the Earth's surface to form. However, the geologists could only guess at how old the rocks actually were.

Clocks in rocks

This all changed when scientists discovered 'clocks in rocks'! **Geologists** found they could measure a special property of the rocks – a property called **radioactivity** – that could tell them how old the rocks actually are.

Geologists use simple hammers to collect rock samples. These samples are then examined in the laboratory with complicated instruments, such as this one, which can measure radioactivity to reveal a rock's age.

A timeline

Geologists have named different periods of time in history to help them date rocks. The oldest rocks are about 4 billion years old, from an age called the Precambrian Period. They are metamorphic rocks from north-west Canada. We know more about conditions on Earth in later periods, from the Cambrian Period (about 540 million years ago) through several more periods to the present Quaternary Period, which began about 1.8 million years ago.

Fossils

Many sedimentary rocks contain fossils. These are impressions of prehistoric life. Some fossilized creatures look like nothing living on the Earth today, so they must have died out a very long time ago. Fossils of extinct animals added to the evidence that most of the Earth's rocks must be very old indeed.

Most of the fossils we find are millions of years old. This is the fossil of a fish that lived 56 million years ago. ⇨

⇦ These ancient sedimentary rocks in Arizona have been worn away by the wind to reveal hundreds of layers.

The atmosphere

The Earth is surrounded by a protective layer of gases, known as the atmosphere. These gases include nitrogen and also oxygen, the gas all life needs in order to live. The atmosphere contains less of these gases the higher you go. At around 100km high, there is no more atmosphere, and space begins.

A protective shield

The atmosphere is a barrier that protects us from a great deal of harm from space. It absorbs dangerous rays from the Sun. Large **meteoroids** and small comets arriving from space also break up when they enter the atmosphere.

⇧ Are **hurricanes** a result of **global warming**? This picture is of Hurricane Andrew approaching the southern coast of the USA, in August 1992.

A climate blanket

Most of the atmosphere is contained within a layer just 10km deep. Much of our weather takes place inside this layer. Heat and water vapour move around the globe inside the atmosphere, giving us our different weather and climate patterns.

Key Concept

24

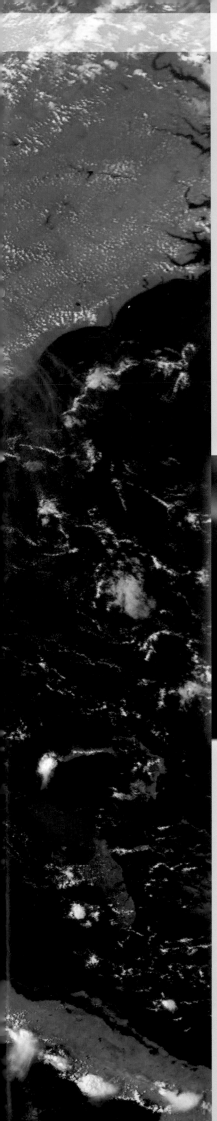

Displays in the atmosphere

Some wonderful sights in the night sky are produced in the atmosphere. Bright flashes of light, called meteors, are caused when tiny bits of comet burn up in the atmosphere. Meteorites are small, harmless chunks of meteoroids. When they travel through the Earth's atmosphere they become spectacular fireballs.

⇧ When small objects from space, such as these meteorites, enter the atmosphere, they burn up and leave a trail behind them.

⇦ The aurorae are multicoloured light displays that take place in the atmosphere. They are caused when particles from the Sun hit the oxygen and nitrogen in the atmosphere, and glow brightly. This is a picture of the Aurora Borealis (Northern Lights), seen over Iceland.

Global warming

Extremes of weather, such as droughts and hurricanes, are sometimes explained as the result of our changing climate, as the Earth warms up. Many people think that this global warming has been caused by human activity. Our cars, planes and factories release too many harmful gases into the atmosphere, damaging it so that it cannot protect us so well. We need to look after our atmosphere so that it can continue to do its job.

Life on Earth

As we have seen, planet Earth is special in many ways. Perhaps its most special quality is that it is a planet upon which many different plants and animals can survive.

⇩ These thick chalk cliffs are made of the skeletons of countless billions of tiny marine lifeforms, which lived more than 100 million years ago.

Life begins

Life first appeared on our planet about 3.5 billion years ago. Simple life was able to change carbon dioxide gas and water into oxygen. Other life forms then developed that made use of this oxygen. About 540 million years ago, at the beginning of the Cambrian Period, the life forms on Earth became more complex and varied, and lots of different plants and animals began to thrive in the sea and on land.

⇧ This is how the Earth may have looked at the beginning of the Cambrian Period, as life on Earth began to flourish.

A suitable environment

There are many different environments on Earth with animals and plants that are particularly suited to them. Life can be found almost everywhere, from blisteringly hot volcanic vents in the depths of the ocean to the freezing world of Antarctica.

⇧ This hot volcanic vent on the sea bed is known as a 'black smoker'. Life may first have developed around these undersea features.

Key Concept

DNA and evolution

All animals and plants contain DNA**. This is a code that sets out how something should look and work. DNA helps all living things to grow and reproduce. If the DNA of an animal or plant changes, it will look and behave differently. This can make it better suited to its environment, and help it to survive. The DNA of life on Earth has been changing for millions of years, which is why so many different types of plants and animals live on our planet. We call these changes** evolution**.**

Earthwatching

Satellites allow us to study the Earth from space. They have shown us a great deal about its continents, seas, ice sheets and atmosphere. We can also use them to watch any changes that affect our planet.

Mapping satellites

Mapping satellites carefully measure shapes on the Earth's surface, from the peaks of the Himalayas to the valleys of California. They have also mapped the ocean floors in great detail. Some satellites can even show what types of **mineral** are in the Earth's rocks.

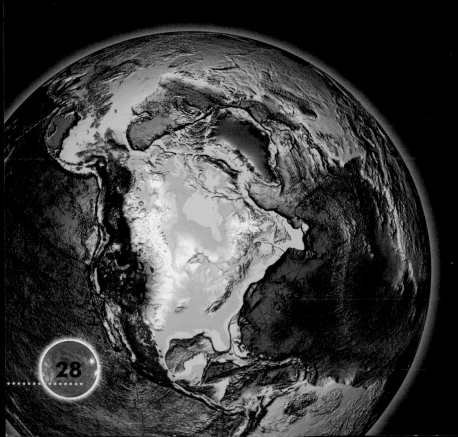

At night, satellites show us just how many people live on our planet, when it is lit up from space with bright city lights, road lights and industrial fires.

Orbiting satellites have mapped the contours of the surface of the Earth and the sea bed.

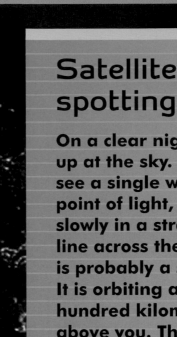
Satellite spotting

On a clear night, look up at the sky. If you see a single white point of light, moving slowly in a straight line across the sky, it is probably a satellite. It is orbiting a few hundred kilometres above you. The International Space Station **can appear very bright, as sunlight glints off its large, shiny panels.**

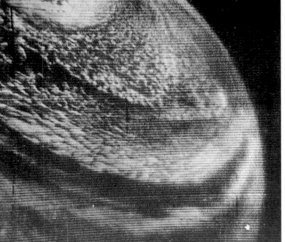

⇧ The first-ever weather satellite image of the Earth was taken in 1960.

Weather satellites

Weather was first monitored from space in 1960. Since then, weather satellites have become very advanced. They can now track clouds and storms, identify rain clouds, see the dust blown out into the atmosphere by volcanoes, and measure the atmosphere's chemical content.

Humans affecting the planet

Tropical rainforests are cleared every year to make way for land upon which farm animals can feed. In 2006, satellites showed that an area of Brazilian rainforest the size of Greece was destroyed in this way. Changes like this harm plant and animal life, damage our climate and could change the way Earth looks for ever. We must all take better care of Earth so that it continues to be one of the most beautiful and life-filled planets in our Solar System..

Glossary

asteroid   a lump of rock in space

Asteroid Belt   a band of space between the planets Mars and Jupiter containing thousands of large asteroids

climate   the average temperature and weather experienced in different parts of the world

comet   a huge ball of ice and dust in space

continent   a large landmass. There are seven continents on Earth: Asia (the largest), Africa, North America, South America, Antarctica, Europe and Australia (the smallest)

continental drift   the movement of the Earth's continents in relation to each other

core   the heaviest, thickest part of a planet, lying at its centre

crater   a large, bowl-shaped pit which has been blasted out of a solid surface by the impact of an asteroid. Volcanoes also have small craters at their tops

density   how heavy an object is compared with its volume

DNA   the substance in the cells of all plant and animal life on Earth. DNA stands for deoxyribonucleic acid

earthquake   a shaking motion in the Earth's crust caused when two plates slide past each other

evolution   the process by which life forms on Earth have changed to survive in their own particular environment

fossil   the preserved remains of prehistoric plants and animals in rock

freshwater   water that does not have much salt. Freshwater is found in most lakes and rivers

geologist   someone who studies the structure of the Earth's crust and its layers

global warming   a gradual rise in the average temperature on Earth

gravity   a force that acts throughout the Universe. The Earth's gravity holds you to its surface, and the Sun's gravity holds the Earth in its orbit. The bigger the object, the more gravity it has

hurricane   a powerful storm of rain clouds hundreds of kilometres wide, with average windspeeds over 100kph

Ice Ages   periods of global cooling lasting around 100 000 years, during which the polar ice caps grow

ice caps   vast, thick sheets of ice covering the Earth's polar regions

International Space Station   a large structure orbiting Earth in which research about space takes place

lava   hot, molten rock which has bubbled up from below a planet's crust

magma   hot, molten rock that is beneath the Earth's crust

mantle   a layer of molten rock between the Earth's crust and its core, about 2900km thick

meteoroid   a small rock in space, usually a chip off an asteroid

mineral   a solid material made of chemicals

molten   something so hot that it is in a melted state

Moon   the Earth's only natural satellite. Other natural satellites are also known as moons (with a small 'm')

orbit   the curved path of a planet or another object round a star, or a moon round a planet

planet   a large, round object orbiting a star

plate   a large segment of the Earth's solid crust

polar regions   the cold areas at the very top and bottom of a planet. Polar regions are cold because they are the areas of a planet that are furthest from the Sun

radioactivity   energy given off by rocks which helps scientists to work out how old the rocks are

saltwater   water that contains a lot of salt. Saltwater is most often found in seas and oceans

satellite   a small object in orbit around a larger object. Man-made satellites are sent up into space to study the Earth

Solar System   our part of space, containing the Sun, the planets and their moons, asteroids and comets

space   everything outside the Earth's atmosphere

Sun   our nearest star, a huge ball of burning gas

Universe   everything there is, to the unimaginably distant reaches of space

volcano   a mountain built up by the eruption of hot, molten rock and piles of ash

weathering   the wearing away of Earth's surface by weather, such as rain and wind